new world
collection

Wise Publications

London / New York / Paris / Sydney / Copenhagen / Berlin / Madrid / Tokyo

Exclusive distributors:
Music Sales Limited
8/9 Frith Street, London W1D 3JB, England.
Music Sales Pty Limited
120 Rothschild Avenue, Rosebery, NSW 2018, Australia.

Order No. AM976899
ISBN 0-7119-9895-7
This book © Copyright 2003 by Wise Publications.

Music arranged by Derek Jones.
Music Engraved by Paul Ewers Music Design.

Front cover main photograph courtesy of Getty Images.
All other photographs courtesy of LFI.

Your Guarantee of Quality:

As publishers, we strive to produce every book
to the highest commercial standards.

The book has been carefully designed to
minimise awkward page turns and to make
playing from it a real pleasure.

Particular care has been given to specifying
acid-free, neutral-sized paper made from pulps which
have not been elemental chlorine bleached.

This pulp is from farmed sustainable forests and
was produced with special regard for the environment.

Throughout, the printing and binding have been
planned to ensure a sturdy, attractive publication
which should give years of enjoyment.

If your copy fails to meet our high standards,
please inform us and we will gladly replace it.

Printed in Malta by Interprint Limited.

www.musicsales.com

all the things she said t.a.t.u. 4

beautiful christina aguilera 13

castles in the sky ian van dahl 30

come into my world kylie minogue 18

complicated avril lavigne 24

don't worry appleton 35

hands clean alanis morissette 42

heaven (piano version) dj sammy 54

hungry kosheen 48

if i fall alice martineau 59

i'm gonna getcha good! shania twain 84

imagine eva cassidy 64

just like a pill pink 68

the ketchup song (asereje) las ketchup 72

king of sorrow sade 78

the last goodbye atomic kitten 91

love letters diana krall 96

the nearness of you norah jones 108

objection (tango) shakira 101

ordinary day vanessa carlton 112

shoot the moon norah jones 117

should i feel that it's over alison moyet 120

stronger sugababes 125

through the rain mariah carey 130

the tide is high (get the feeling) atomic kitten 137

whenever, wherever shakira 142

wrong impression natalie imbruglia 154

you'll never be alone anastacia 148

all the things she said

Words & Music by Sergei Galoyan, Trevor Horn, Martin Kierszenbaum, Elena Kiper & Valerij Polienko

All the things she said, all the things she said, run-ning through my head, run-ning through my head, all the things she said. This is not e-nough.

1. I'm in

se-ri-ous shit, I feel to-tal-ly lost,_ if I'm ask-ing for help_ it's on-ly be-cause_

be - ing with you_ has op - ened my eyes. Could I ev - er be - lieve such a per - fect sur - prise? I keep

ask - ing my - self, won - der - ing how._ I keep clos - ing my eyes, but I can't block you out. Wan - na

fly to a place_ where it's just you and me,_ no - bo - dy else,_ so we can be free,_

(no - bo - dy else,_ so we can be free.)_ All the things she said, all the things she said, run - ning through my

2. And I'm all mixed up feel-ing corn-ered and rushed. They

say it's my fault, but I want her so much, wan-na fly her a-way where the sun and the rain_ come in

ov - er my face, wash a - way all the shame. When they stop and stare, don't wor - ry me_ 'cause I'm

feel - ing for her____ what she's feel - ing for me.____ I can

try to pre-tend, I can try to for - get,_ but it's driv - ing me mad,_ go - ing out of my

head.____ All the things she said, all the things she said, run - ning through my

All the things she said, all the things she said.

All the things she said, all the things she said.

All the things she said, all the things she said, all the things she

said, all the things she said. She said, all the things she said, all the things she said.

Mo - ther, look - ing at me, tell me what do you see? Yes, I lost my mind.__
Dad - dy, look - ing at me, will I ev - er be free? Have I crossed the line?__

D.S. al Coda

Coda

All the things she said, all the things she said, all the things she

said. All the things she said, all the things she said, all the things she said.

beautiful

Words & Music by Linda Perry

(Don't look at me) *Vocal ad lib.*

1. Ev - 'ry day__ is so
2. To all your friends you're de -

I am beau-ti-ful,___ in ev-'ry sin-gle way.__ Yes,
You are beau-ti-ful,___ in ev-'ry sin-gle way.__ Yes,
We are beau-ti-ful,___ in ev-'ry sin-gle way.__ Yes,

words can't bring me___ down.___ Oh,___ no.___
words can't bring you___ down.___ Oh,___ no.___
words can't bring us___ down.___ Oh,___ no.___

So don't you bring me down__ to-day.

come into my world

Words & Music by Cathy Dennis & Rob Davis

L.H. 8va bassa throughout

Come,___ come,___ come in - to___ my world.

watch - ing ov - er____ you._____ 2. And I've

been____ such a long time____ wait - ing for some - one____ I could call____ my
(Verse 3 see block lyric)

own.____ I've been chas - ing the life I've____ dreamed, and now I'm____

____ home._____

21

Verse 3:
Take these lips that were made for kissing
And this heart that will see you through
And these hands that were made to touch and feel you.

So free your love.
Hear me, I'm calling.

complicated

Words & Music by Lauren Christy, David Alspach, Graeme Edwards & Avril Lavigne

Moderate Pop

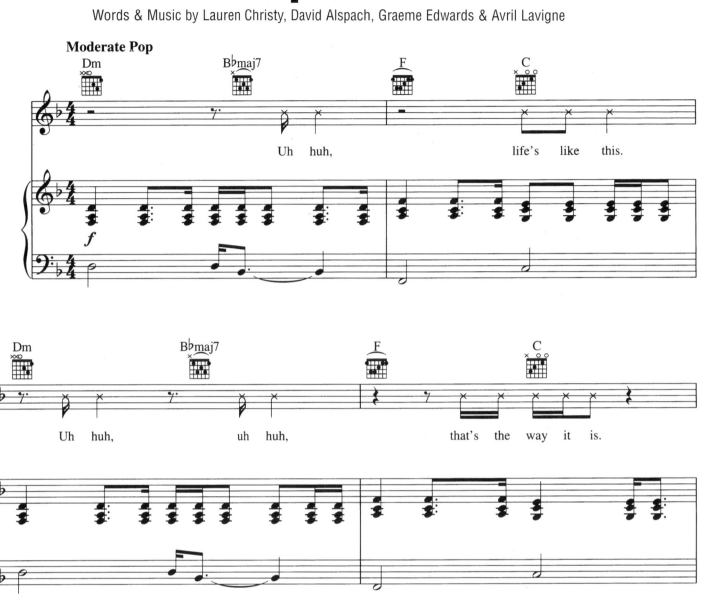

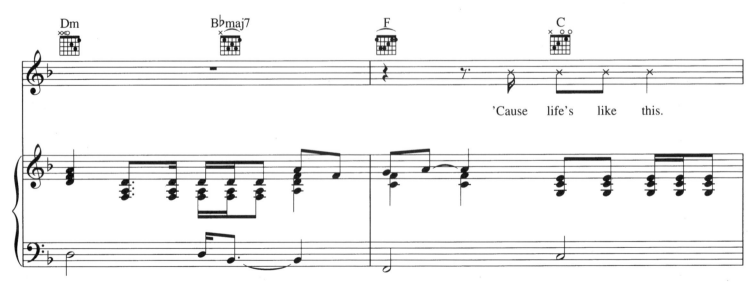

no, no, no, no, no, no, no, no,

no, no, no, no. Chill out, what cha yell - in' for?

D.S. al Coda

CODA

try'n' to be cool. You look like a fool to me._____ Tell me ___

why'd you have to go and make things so com - pli - cat - ed? See the way you're

castles in the sky

Words & Music by Erik Vanspauwen, Christophe Chantzis & Martine Theeuwen

31

don't worry

Words & Music by D. Hastings, Natalie Appleton & Craigie Dodds

but I think___ that   we missed out.___
a place   that we could meet?___

So I've sung___ this   song for you___
And you see this face with - in   your face and I   stayed a -

and I just want___ you   to say   to me...___
- way   but I'm back___   to hear you say...___

Don't wor - ry 'cause I'll al - ways be there _____ for you._

In the hea - vens _____ a - bove.

Don't wor - ry 'cause I'll al - ways be there _____ for you._

1.

Al - ways be there.

Al - ways be there.__
(Bro - ken man.)__

(Vocal ad lib.)

Yeah,__ yeah._____

41

hands clean

Words & Music by Alanis Morissette

and ov - er - look___ this sup - pos - ed crime.___

We'll fast - for - ward to a few years___ la - ter and,

and no - one knows ex - cept the both of___ us.___ And I have hon - oured your re -

-quest for___ si - lence___ and you have washed___ your hands___ clean of___ this.

To Coda

44

45

Verse 2:
You're essentially an employee and I like you having to depend on me
You're kind of my protégé and one day you'll say you learned all you know from me
I know you depend on me like a young thing would to a guardian
I know you sexualize me like a young thing would and I think I like it.
Ooh this could get messy
But you don't seem to mind
Ooh don't go telling everybody
And overlook this supposed crime.

Verse 3:
Just make sure you don't tell on me especially to members of your family
We best keep this to ourselves and not tell any members of our inner posse
I wish I could tell the world 'cause you're such a pretty thing when you're done up properly
I might want to marry you one day if you watch that weight and you keep your firm body.
Ooh this could be messy and
Ooh I don't seem to mind
Ooh don't go telling everybody
And overlook this supposed crime.

We'll fastforward to a few years later   *etc.*

hungry

Words & Music by Darren Beale, Mark Morrison & Sian Evans

1. You're like a child with old eyes,
(Verse 2 see block lyric)

cy - ni - cal and sen - si - ble, al - ways full of sur - prise.

Are you hun - gry_____ for a lit - tle more__ than what you've had be - fore?__ Are you hun - gry_____ for a taste of life,__ wet your ap - pe - tite.__ Are you hun - gry?_____

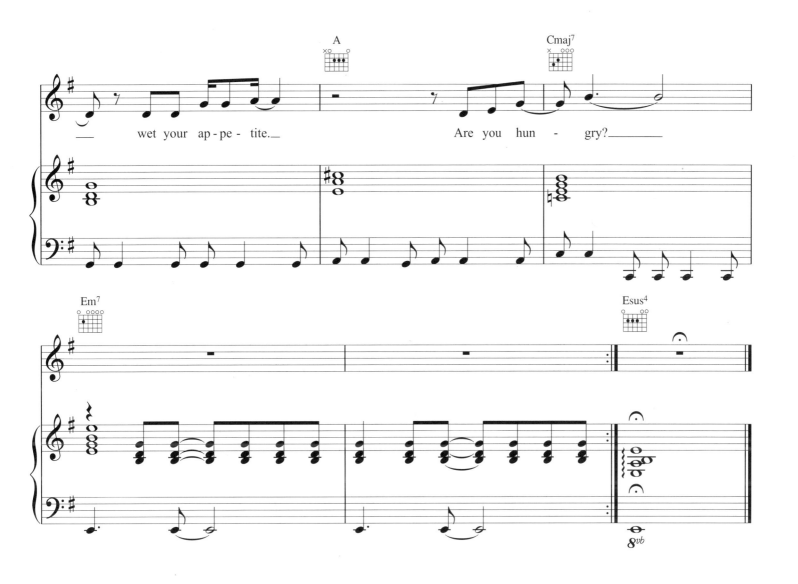

wet your ap - pe - tite.___   Are you hun - gry?_____

Verse 2:
Now give me this mountainside
Cool water, to lie beside
Give me these two strong eyes
To see the difference between truth and lies
Oh, give me this feeling
When you kiss me baby, every day and every night
That's all I need, yes
Everything else gonna be alright.

Are you hungry *etc.*

heaven

Words & Music by Bryan Adams & Jim Vallance

if i fall

Words & Music by Alice Martineau

searching my his - t'ry for a rea - son. I'm all a - lone,

I've nev - er felt so a - lone. A - lone If I cry

D.S. al Coda

Coda

Guitar

I nev - er felt so a - lone,

imagine

Words & Music by John Lennon

-low us,___ a- bove_ us on - ly_ sky.

Im- ag - ine all_ the peo - ple_____ liv - ing_____ for_ to - day.

You,_____ you may say_____ that I'm_

_ a dream - er, but I'm not the on - ly one.___

Verse 2:
Imagine there's no countries
It isn't hard to do
Nothing to kill or die for
And no religion too
Imagine all the people living life in peace.

Verse 3:
Imagine no possessions
I wonder if you can
No need for greed or hunger
A brotherhood of man
Imagine all the people sharing all the world.

just like a pill

Words & Music by Dallas Austin & Alecia Moore

71

the ketchup song (asereje)

Music & Lyrics by Francisco Manuel Ruiz Gomez

feel - ing rea - dy look - ing fine, vie - ne die - go rum - be - an - do.

With the ma - gic in his eyes, check - ing ev - 'ry girl in sight,

groov - ing like he does the mam - bo. And he's the

man all - i en la dis - co, play - ing sex - y, feel - ing hot - ter. He's the

jè de je-be tu de je-be-re sei - bi-u-nou - va, ma-ja-vi an de

bu - gui an de bui-di-di - pi. A - se - re - jè ja de

jè de je-be tu de je-be-re sei - bi-u-nou - va, ma-ja-vi an de

bu - gui an de bui-di-di - pi. A - se - re - jè ja de

je de je-be tu de je-be-re sei-bi-u-nou-va, ma-ja-vi an de

bu-gui an de bui-di-di-pi.   A-se-re-

A na na   na na na na na na

na na na.   A na na   na na na na na   now._____   A na na

Verse 2:
Many thanks it's brujeria
How he comes and disappears
Every move will hypnotise you
Some will call it chuleria
Others say that it's the real
Rastafari afrogitano.

And he's the man alli en la disco
Playing sexy feeling hotter
He's the King bailando et ritmo ragatanga
And the D.J. that he knows well
On the spot always around twelve
Plays the mix that diego mezcla con la salsa
Y la baila and he dances y la canta.

Aserejè ja de jè de jebe *etc.*

77

king of sorrow

Words & Music by Sade Adu, Stuart Matthewman, Andrew Hale & Paul Denman

rem - nants of joy___ and di - sas - ter: ___ what am I___

___ sup - posed___ to do?___ 2. I want to cook___ you a soup that
(Verse 3 see block lyric)

warms your soul;___ but no - thing would change, no - thing would

change at all. It's just a day___ that brings___ it all a - bout; just an-oth-

- er day,___ and no-thing's a - ny good.___ *Instrumental*

I'm the king____ of sor -

row mm,___ yeah,___ the king of sor - row,___ mm___

Verse 3:
I suppose I could just walk away.
Will I disappoint my future if I stay?

It's just a day that brings it all about *etc.*

i'm gonna getcha good!

Words & Music by Shania Twain & R.J. Lange

To Coda

Verse 3:
I've already planned it
Here's how it's gonna be
I'm gonna love you
And you're gonna fall in love with me.

So don't try to run. *etc.*

the last goodbye

Words & Music by Tor Erik Hermansen, Hallgeir Rustan, Mikkel Eriksen,
Danny Poku, Espen Lind & Amund Bjorklund

1. Ain't no head-lights on the road to-night, ev-'ry-bo-dy here is sleep-ing tight.
(Verse 2 see block lyric)

Ain't no-bo-dy gon-na find us here, we'll dis - ap - pear.

'cause we could-n't seem to find a way___ for love___ to stay.___

If you had a-no-ther night to give___ I would have a-no-ther night to live.___

But you're nev-er gon-na see me cry the last___ good-bye.___

(Last good-bye.)

Verse 2:
Is it cloudy where you are tonight?
Are the neon lights shining bright?
Are you looking for a place to stay to get away?
And the days are horses down the hill
Running fast with no time to kill
And the truth is that we'll never know where love will flow
Aim high, shoot low
(You gotta aim high and shoot low baby).

Ain't no headlights on the road tonight *etc.*

love letters

Words by Edward Heyman
Music by Victor Young

love you write. I me-mo-rise ev-'ry line,

I kiss the name that you sign,

and dar-ling__ then I read a-gain, right from the start;

love let-ters straight from your heart.

objection (tango)

Words & Music by Shakira & Lester Mendez

1. It's not her fault that she's so ir-re-sis-ta-ble,_
(Verse 2 see block lyric)

but all the dam-age she's caused is-n't fix-a-ble._

Ev-'ry twen-ty sec-onds you re-

-peat her___ name but when it comes to me,___

meant to be.__ But you can try it, re - hearse it or train like a horse. But don't you

count on me,__ oh, don't you count on me__ boy.

F#5

D.S. al Coda

Ob -

Verse 2:
Next to her cheap silicon I look minimal.
That's why, in front of your eyes, I'm invisible
But you gotta know small things also count
You'd better put your feet on the ground
And see what it's about.

So objection, I don't wanna be the exception *etc.*

the nearness of you

Words by Ned Washington
Music by Hoagy Carmichael

ordinary day

Words & Music by Vanessa Carlton

Moderately slow ♩. = 69

Verse:

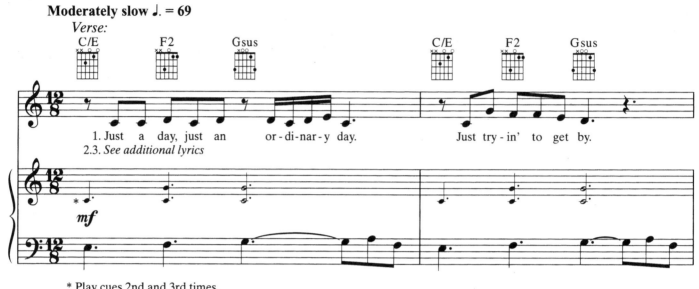

1. Just a day, just an or-di-nar-y day. Just try-in' to get by.
2.3. *See additional lyrics*

* *Play cues 2nd and 3rd times.*

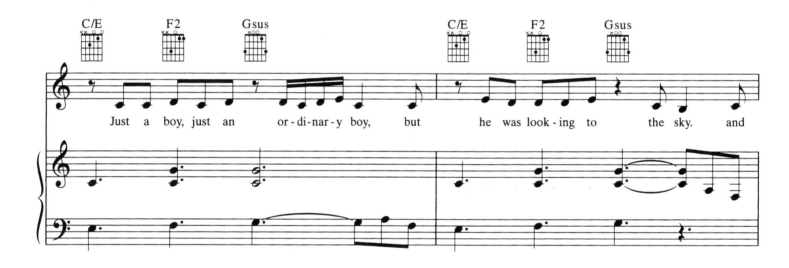

Just a boy, just an or-di-nar-y boy, but he was look-ing to the sky. and

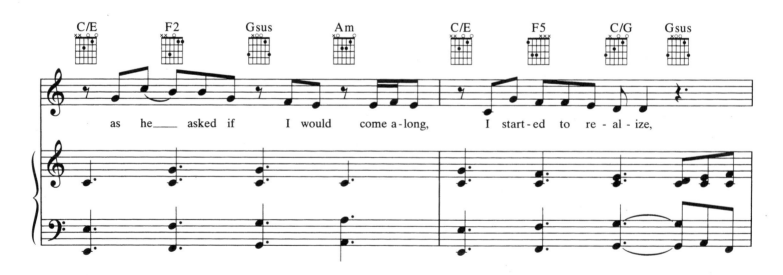

as he___ asked if I would come a-long, I start-ed to re-al-ize,

Verse 2:
And as he spoke, he spoke ordinary words,
Though they did not feel.
For I felt what I had not felt before
And you'd swear those words could heal.
And as I looked up into those eyes,
His vision borrows mine.
And I know he's no stranger
For I feel I've held him for all of time.
And he said...
(To Chorus:)

Verse 3:
Just a dream, just an ordinary dream
As I wake in bed.
And that boy, that ordinary boy,
Was it all in my head?
Didn't he ask if I would come along.
It all seemed so real.
But as I looked to the door,
I saw the boy standing there with a deal.
And he said...
(To Chorus:)

shoot the moon

Word & Music by Jesse Harris

1. The sum-mer days____ are gone____
(Verses 2 see block lyrics, verse 3 instr. til *)

____ too soon; you shoot the moon and miss com-plete-ly.____

Verse 2:
Now the fall is here again
You can't begin to give in, its all over
When the snows come rolling through
You're rolling too with some new lover
Will you think of times you've told me
That you knew the reason
Why we had to each be lonely?
It was just the season.

Verse 3:
(Instrumental)
Will you think of times you've told me
That you knew the reason
Why we had to each be lonely?
It was just the season.

should i feel that it's over

Words & Music by Alison Moyet & Pete Glenister

stronger

Words & Music by Jony Lipsey, Marius De Vries, Felix Howard,
Keisha Buchanan, Mutya Buena, Heidi Range

and fi-nal-ly_ I'm get-ting strong-er.

You'll come to see_

just what I can be,_____ I'm get-ting strong-er

1.
Synth.

2.
I did-n't know what I had to do, I just knew I was_ a-lone.

through the rain

Words & Music by Mariah Carey & Lionel Cole

136

the tide is high (get the feeling)

Words & Music by John Holt, Howard Barrett, Tyrone Evans, Bill Padley & Jem Godfrey

I'm gon-na be your_ num-ber one. Num - ber one. My num-ber one.__

Num - - ber one. (Whisper) Number one. one._____

Ev - 'ry time that I get the feel - ing, you give me some-thing to be - lieve in.

Ev - 'ry time that I got you near me, I know the way that I want it to be.__

who gives up just___ like that,___ oh no___ woh. The

tide is___ high but I'm hold - ing on; I'm gon - na be your___ num - ber one. The

tide is___ high but I'm hold - ing on; I'm gon - na be your___ num - ber one.

Verse 2:
Every girl wants you to be her man
But I'll wait right here till it's my turn
I'm not the kind of girl who gives up just like that
Oh no.

whenever, wherever

Words by Shakira & Gloria Estefan
Music by Shakira & Tim Mitchell

Verse 2:
Lucky that my lips not only mumble
They spill kisses like a fountain
Lucky that my breasts are small and humble
So you don't confuse them with mountains
Lucky I have strong legs like my mother
To run for cover when I need it
And these two eyes are for no other
The day you leave will cry a river
Le do le le le le, le do le le le le
At your feet, I'm at your feet.

Whenever, wherever   *etc.*

you'll never be alone

Words & Music by Anastacia, Sam Watters & Louis Biancaniello

Verse 2:
Hopeless to describe
The way I feel for you
No matter how I try
Words would never do
I looked into your eyes to find
As long as love is alive
There ain't nothing
We can't make it through.
Anytime, or if only for a while
Don't worry
Make a wish
I'll be there to see you smile, ooooh.

Hold on *etc.*

wrong impression

Words & Music by Natalie Imbruglia & Gary Clark

Was-n't try'n to pull you in the wrong di - rec - tion. All I wan-na do is try to make a con - nec - tion,

Repeat ad lib. to fade

yeah,   of love.   I

Verse 2:
Falling out, falling out
Have you ever wondered
If this was ever more than a crazy idea
Falling out, falling out
Have you ever wondered
What we could've been, if you'd only let me in.

I want you
But I want you to understand
I miss you
I love you.

Didn't want to leave you with the wrong impression *etc.*